Invaders & Settlers

KEVIN JANE

ACKNOWLEDGEMENTS

The author and publishers would like to thank the following for permission to reproduce photographs and other materials:

Aerofilms Limited	4; 6; 12
Archäologisches Landesmuseum der Christian - Albrechts - Universität Schloss Gottorf	17
The Ashmolean Museum, Oxford	cover; 15; 27
Avoncroft Museum of Buildings, Bromsgrove, Worcestershire	6
By permission of The British Library	21; 28
Courtesy of the Trustees of The British Museum	cover; 15; 23 (from the plan appearing in *The Sutton Hoo Ship Burial*, Angela Care Evans, British Museum Press, 1989); 27
C. M. Dixon Colour Photo Library	cover; title page; 11; 25; 28; 30; 33-35; 38; 39; 41
Colchester Museums	9
Michael Holford	title page; 5; 7; 14; 15; 31; 34; 35; 38; 39; 42-47
Ronald Sheridan/Ancient Art and Architecture Collection	title page; 1; 4; 8; 12; 15; 24; 27; 28; 31; 39; 42; 46; 47
St. Edmundsbury Borough Council, Leisure Services	19
Society of Antiquaries of London	5
STB/Still Moving	25
York Archaeological Trust Picture Library	36; 37

The publishers have made every effort to contact copyright holders but this has not always been possible. If any have been overlooked we will be pleased to make any necessary arrangements.

First published 1992 by Folens Limited, Dunstable and Dublin.
Folens Limited, Albert House, Apex Business Centre, Boscombe Road, Dunstable LU5 4RL, England.

ISBN 1 85276108-3

Cover Design: Hybert Design & Type.

Illustrators: Ian McGill and Jeffery Burn of Graham Cameron Illustration
                  Keith Allison of Marquee Moon Design
                  Jillian Luff of Bitmap Graphics

Printed in Singapore by Craft Print.

CONTENTS

... a flight of pilums hurtled into the swaying horde of tribesmen, spreading death and confusion wherever the iron heads struck.

1. The Legions Invade

In AD 43 the Emperor Claudius ordered the legions to invade Britain and make it a province of the Roman Empire. Merchants and traders had discovered that Britain was rich in gold, silver, lead, tin, corn, meat, hunting dogs, skins and wool. Prisoners could become slaves back in Rome and taxes could be collected to help run the vast Roman Empire.

Look for the Roman warships engraved on this column.

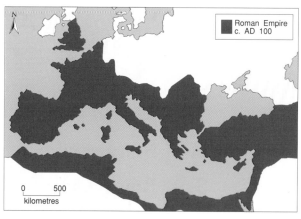

Name the countries the Romans occupied in AD 100.

Rome was a vast, wealthy city with beautiful buildings, streets and shops, theatres and entertainments, a good water supply and a population as large as Birmingham today. Why, then, were the Romans interested in Britain? Merchants and traders had told them of the country but they were suspicious of the weather and Britain's warlike people. They wanted to see the country for themselves.

The first invasion came in 55 BC, led by Julius Caesar. His small army defeated tribes in the south east of Britain, but it did not try to capture the country. There were no more attacks on Britain for nearly 100 years.

Why would Maiden Castle have been difficult to attack?

Archaeologists have discovered many fragments of uniform and equipment which tell us what the Roman soldier looked like. He wore battledress made from metal and leather.

Remains from the attack on Maiden Castle. Look for clues to explain how these three people died.

At this time, the Roman army was the finest fighting machine in the world. Part of the army was made of citizens of Rome who were grouped into legions. There were over 5 000 legionaries altogether. They were well-armed and well-trained fighting men. They were also skilled engineers and craftsmen because they had to build roads, bridges and forts. The rest of the army was made up of auxilia - tribes which the Romans had defeated and forced to fight on their side. Their job in battle was to protect the legions by fighting in front of, or to the side of them.

The conquest of Britain was not easy. The hill-fort, Maiden Castle, in Dorset was the scene of a savage fight. On the inner bank of the fort there were high wooden walls. From these walls the defenders fired missiles at the attackers. The Romans used a ballista, which was a huge crossbow. They also had slingers who shot stones collected from nearby Chesil beach. Many people died during the fierce hand-to-hand fighting at Maiden Castle.

By AD 80 the Romans had conquered most of Britain and the country became peaceful. The Romans were good rulers - they allowed the tribes to keep their own customs and worship their own gods. But they also encouraged the chiefs to dress, eat and live like the Romans.

? Roman invasion

Use the information available to you in this unit.

1. Why did the Romans attack Britain?
2. Where was there a bitter battle? How do we know?
3. Why do you think the Romans were able to defeat the Britons?
4. Describe the uniform and equipment of a typical Roman soldier.

One must remember we are dealing with barbarians ... The climate is wretched, with its frequent rains and mists, but there is no extreme cold ...

Imagine life in a Celtic home.

2. Britannia

The people who lived in Britain at the time of the Roman invasion were divided up into tribes. Each tribe ruled different areas of the country. The people were called Celts and had settled in Britain about 2 500 years before. This time is called the Iron Age because the Celts found out how to make iron tools and weapons. This was one of the most important discoveries ever made.

The tribes lived in scattered villages. Their huts were usually made of wattle and daub - twigs which were woven together and plastered with mud or clay. Sometimes they were made of stone. The huts had thatched roofs.

Life was hard for the Celtic tribes. They were mainly farmers who grew, gathered or hunted for their food. They were also fierce warriors who were often at war with each other, raiding their neighbours for cattle or slaves. For this reason they needed to defend themselves and built huge earthworks known as hill-forts. These were built on top of hills and had banks and ditches and wooden walls. The entrances to the hill-forts were made as strong as possible to make it difficult for attackers to get in. The hill-forts were sometimes the homes of important chiefs and their families. Others were simple meeting places. The larger hill-forts were like small towns with streets and houses, places for worship and workshops for the craftsmen.

Look for evidence of the ditches and banks which would have surrounded this hill-fort, protecting the Celtic tribe from their neighbours.

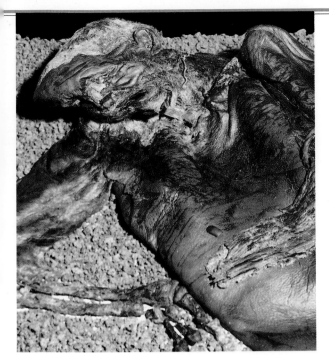

The remains of "Pete Marsh", the Lindow man.

moustaches, which acted like strainers when they drank. The warriors' favourite weapon was a long sword or spear and they often fought naked!

Women wore floor-length skirts and cloaks. The cloth was woven on upright looms in their dwellings. Their hair was often worn in long plaits. Neck rings were popular and bronze pins fastened the clothes together. Both men and women wore leather shoes.

Digging for peat in Cheshire some workmen accidentally discovered half a human body. Tests proved that the body was that of a man who had died over 2 000 years ago. The peat had preserved the body. "Pete Marsh", as the man was nicknamed, was a Celt.

The archaeologists did some detective work on the remains of the body. They discovered he had ginger hair, a moustache and a beard which had been neatly trimmed. His fingernails were trimmed and cut, which suggests that he did not do rough work. He had been strangled with a knotted cord which had broken his neck, and his skull had been fractured by a heavy blow. The contents of his stomach revealed that his last meal was of partly burned barley cakes and a porridge mixture!

The Celts were great show-offs. This was displayed in their appearance and the style of their clothes. Men wore their hair long - it was stiffened into spikes and scraped back like a horse's mane. They were also fond of

Celtic cloth was usually brightly coloured and chequered like tartan.

 The Celts

Read through this unit.

1. Describe the people that the Romans found when they invaded Britain. Draw your own pictures of their clothes.
2. Why do you think the Lindow man died? Was it a sacrifice to the gods? Do you think he was a captured slave or a criminal? Write his story.

I am fighting as an ordinary person for my lost freedom, my bruised body, and my outraged daughters ... Let the men live in slavery if they will.

3.

What sort of person does Boudicca seem from this statue?

Boudicca

The story of Boudicca's revolt starts in what we now call Norfolk. In these times the Iceni tribe lived there, ruled by their king, Prasutagus. In AD 60 he died, leaving half of his wealth to his wife, Boudicca, and half to the Roman Emperor in the hope that the Romans would leave his wife and people to live in peace.

The Romans, however, were not content with this arrangement. Tax collectors looted his lands, whipped his wife and assaulted his daughters. Outraged, the Iceni tribe revolted.

Other tribes the Romans had angered joined in the revolt. The start of the revolt was swift and terrifying. The Celtic tribes were led by Boudicca and their first targets were the country villas of wealthy Romans. The villas were destroyed and their occupants slaughtered. The tribes moved towards Colchester. The people of Colchester were poorly armed and the end came quickly. Boudicca surrounded the temple and burned down the town. The Celts attacked the temple and destroyed the Roman cemetery, breaking tombstones and statues.

Within a short time the revolt had spread. Chelmsford and St. Albans were burned. Now the whole Roman future in Britain was at stake. The Roman governor, Suetonius Paulinus, was with the main Roman army far away in Anglesey fighting the Druids. These were powerful Celtic priests. When Suetonius heard the news that Britain was in revolt, he marched towards London.

Celtic tribes in Britain.

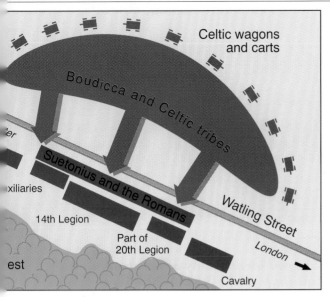

The final battle between Boudicca leading the Celts and Suetonius leading the Romans.

London was a Roman creation - a trading centre of great wealth and many thousands of people. When Suetonius arrived he realised he could not defend it against Boudicca's army. So he abandoned it, much to the horror and fear of the London people. Boudicca's army descended on London and burned it to the ground. Deaths were estimated at 70 000.

It was clear that eventually Boudicca and Suetonius would meet for a final battle. Archaeologists do not know exactly where this battle took place; only that it was somewhere along Watling Street, a road running from Wroxeter to London. The Romans had 10 000 men, while the Celts had many times that number. But Roman discipline won the day against a bloodthirsty rabble. The Celts could not use their weapons when they were tightly packed together. They were easy prey for the Romans' short swords and shields. 400 Romans died in the battle but 80 000 Celts were killed! The revolt was over - Boudicca had no option but to commit suicide and the Roman grip on Britain became tighter.

❓ Boudicca's revolt

Look again at this unit.

1. Make a map showing the important events in Boudicca's revolt.
2. What was the cause of the revolt?
3. If you had been Suetonius what would you have done about London?
4. The final battle was decisive. Why? What do you think the effect would have been on Celtic tribes?

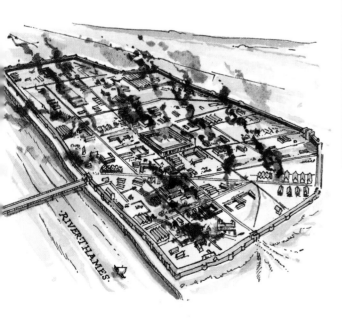

Boudicca's army sets fire to London. A Roman writer tells how the rebels, "could not wait to hang, cut throats, burn and crucify".

Why do you think the tombstone of this Roman cavalry officer has been broken?

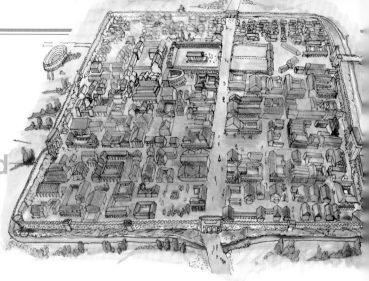

> If you can call it a city where it has no state buildings, no training ground, no theatre and no market square, where it has no running water.

4. Roman Towns

A Roman wrote the words at the top of this page to describe a poor city in Greece. They give us an idea of what a Roman thought a town or city should have. The Romans liked living in towns and built them in every country that they conquered. Although they were much smaller than many of our towns today, they were certainly larger, richer and more carefully planned and built than anything the Celts living in Britain were used to.

The towns grew out of Roman military camps. Roman soldiers had money to spend and so traders and merchants set up their workshops and shops near the barracks.

Why are these Roman towns in good locations?

Can you identify any of the structures or buildings in the Roman town of Colchester?

The camps were situated in places where the local tribes might cause trouble, but eventually the people became peaceful and adopted a more Roman way of life. Towns were also built in valley locations where the soil for farming was good, near river crossings or on sites which had good communications.

Many of our towns today began as Roman settlements. There are clues in their names. If the modern name ends in "chester", "caster" or "cester", it is likely that it was originally a Roman military base. The word comes from **castrum** which means "Army Camp". Eventually they became properly planned towns with the facilities that Romans were used to.

Roman craftsmen, butchers and bakers worked in open shops above which they also lived.

Roman towns

Read the information on Roman towns.

1. How did the Romans choose where to build their towns?
2. What did all Roman towns have?
3. Which Roman town do you live nearest to?
4. What do you think about the style of Roman town planning?

What did the towns look like?

Archaeologists have discovered that many Roman towns followed a similar pattern and contained similar buildings.

1. From the artist's picture of Colchester find:
    - the main gates to the town;
    - town walls and ditches for protection;
    - the square or rectangular building plots;
    - baths where Romans could meet, swim and clean themselves;
    - temples for worshipping different gods;
    - the Forum which was the market place in the centre of the town where most of the business was done;
    - the Basilica which was joined to the Forum and held the government offices and law courts;
    - the Amphitheatre where gladiators and animals fought in front of an audience.

Shops in Roman times

Look at the three pictures of Roman shops. They were carved in stone in Roman times.

1. For each decide:
    - what goods are on sale in the shop;
    - who is the shopkeeper and who is the customer.
2. Describe the differences between our shops today and shops in Roman times.

5. Roman Frontiers and Roads

Hadrian's Wall was 4.5 metres high and 3 metres wide.

it was covered in dense forests. Here, the local tribes could hide and make it very difficult for the Romans to conquer them. The Romans had to build over 100 camps and forts where the most rebellious tribes lived.

In Scotland (the Romans called it Caledonia), they failed to conquer the warlike Picts because the landscape was so wild. So, in AD 122 the Roman Emperor Hadrian ordered that a wall should be built to stop the Picts attacking - a wall that was built from one side of the country to the other.

Some of our modern roads follow the old lines of the straight Roman roads.

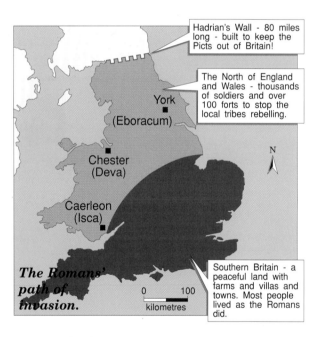

Hadrian's Wall - 80 miles long - built to keep the Picts out of Britain!

The North of England and Wales - thousands of soldiers and over 100 forts to stop the local tribes rebelling.

York (Eboracum)

Chester (Deva)

Caerleon (Isca)

N

The Romans' path of invasion.

0   100
kilometres

Southern Britain - a peaceful land with farms and villas and towns. Most people lived as the Romans did.

Once the Romans decided to make Britain part of the Roman Empire it was important to stop the local Celtic tribes from rebelling. The Romans quickly conquered the south of Britain where the land was fairly flat. Some of the tribes were friendly and adapted to the new way of life easily. In the north and in Wales the countryside is hilly and in those days

The wall that Hadrian ordered the legions to build was the northern boundary of the Roman Empire. Along the 80 miles of the wall, 17 forts were built. At every mile between the forts were smaller forts called milecastles and between these were signal turrets. On the English side of the wall there was a deep ditch called the Vallum. Much of the wall, milecastles and forts still exist today.

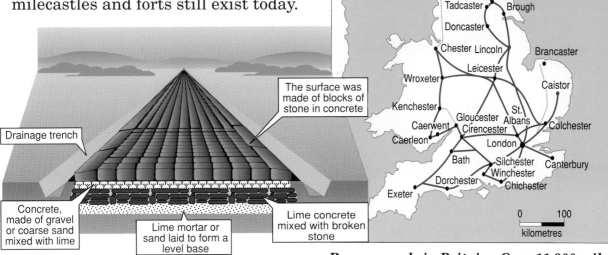

Try to make your own model of a Roman road.

Roman roads in Britain. Over 11 900 miles were built.

It was important for the Romans to be able to move their army and its baggage around the country quickly. They built their first proper roads in Britain, which connected their forts and later joined up the towns and cities. They built the roads as straight as they could so that travel was made as quick as possible.

The roads were built a little above the level of the ground and the road surface was curved slightly so that rainwater ran off into ditches on either side. The surface was made of stones rammed hard on top of concrete. The trees, bushes and vegetation on either side were cut down to avoid an ambush.

Hadrian's Wall

Use the evidence in this unit.

1. Why was Hadrian's Wall built?
2. Draw a diagram of Hadrian's Wall showing:
   - a milecastle;
   - a signal turret;
   - the Vallum.
3. Why were the roads built? How do we know they were very well constructed?

Britain under the Romans

Look at the map showing roughly the peaceful areas of conquered Britain and the more unsettled areas where the Roman army was still needed to settle the local tribes.

1. Which areas had the Romans successfully conquered?
2. Which areas were outside Roman control?

... eat they did, at a small table drawn close before the hearth ... and wine ... that tasted of sunshine and the south, in flasks of wonderful coloured glass.

6. Roman Lifestyle

Only two or three fragments of clothing have survived in Britain from Roman times. However, wall paintings and sculptures show us the style of Roman clothing and their appearance.

Men wore under-tunics that reached to their knees with a belt around the middle. Important men wore a toga. This was a semi-circular piece of cloth which was thrown over the left shoulder and then wrapped around the body. Leather sandals or shoes were worn. Men had their hair cut short.

Women wore underclothes that resembled a bra and pants. Over these they wore a short tunic and then a longer over-dress with sleeves. Cloaks with hoods were popular. Women's hairstyles favoured tight curls and buns held in place with pins. Necklaces, brooches, rings and bracelets were common, and perfume was often worn. Like men, Roman women wore leather sandals.

What shape has the Roman glass vessel been made as?

Roman artefacts

Look at these pictures of Roman artefacts and remains.

1. See if you can identify each one from the clue:
   - for keeping feet warm and dry, made of leather;
   - to wear on the wrist;
   - for plucking out hairs;
   - for spending and buying a new toga perhaps?
   - in the baths - one for oil and two for scraping the body clean;
   - for decorating the fingers;
   - a floor covering made of tiny stones laid in beautiful designs;
   - filled with olive oil to light your way;
   - for smoothing wood;
   - for holding hair in place;
   - a box for drugs and medical instruments.

Studying Roman artefacts and remains helps us to understand the quality of their life. Think about the materials these objects have been made from.

The Goths broke into Rome and never since has a Roman ruled in Britain.

7. Sea Pirates!

Which seas did the invaders cross on their way to Britain?

Around AD 400 Rome itself was being attacked by tribes of warriors from Germany, Denmark and Eastern Europe. Rome had to recall the legions from Britain to defend itself. This left England, by now a wealthy country, open to attack. The Picts invaded from Scotland and the Scots came from Ireland. Tribes of Angles, Saxons and Jutes came across the sea from Denmark, Holland and Germany. When Britain asked for help, the message from Rome was that they should defend themselves.

Without Roman protection Britain was easy prey to the fierce pirates who came in search of jewellery, gold and slaves.

At first the pirates came to raid the coastal areas. Later they decided to try to conquer Britain, to settle and farm the country. They came in long, sleek rowing boats which had no sails. The boats held between 60 and 80 people and needed 30 men to row them.

By AD 650 it was the Saxons who had captured most of Britain except for the North, Wales and Cornwall. They looked for places to live which would give them rich soil, fresh water and the materials they would need to build their small settlements and farmsteads.

Archaeologists have pieced together evidence to give us an idea of Saxon weapons and armour. The more important warriors wore iron helmets on their heads. Some wore armour made of metal rings sewn on to a tight leather jacket - a jerkin. They protected themselves with round shields made of wood, often covered in leather and decorated. The boss, a raised iron cup in the centre of the shield, protected the warrior's hands. Saxons carried long swords, spears and knives which could be used for many purposes.

The Saxons

Look carefully at this unit.

1. Why did the Saxons raid Britain?
2. Draw your own map showing the tribes which attacked Britain and where they raided.
3. Why were Saxon raids successful?
4. The Saxons did not have it all their own way - the Britons fought back. Find out about a warrior king called Arthur!

What would this Saxon soldier use to attack an enemy? What would help to protect him?

How many oars were used to power this Saxon longboat?

In the hall of the King of the Geats, a hundred men listened. Almost silence. The cat fire hissed and spat, golden-eyed tapestries winked out of the gloom.

8. Saxon Settlement and Buildings

By AD 650 most of Britain had been conquered by the Saxons. The chiefs became kings and ruled over areas of land called kingdoms. Eventually, because some kings were more powerful than others, three great kingdoms emerged - Northumbria, Mercia and Wessex. Each was ruled by a powerful king. However, the country was less populated than it is today - it had only between one and two million people.

Many of our towns and villages today take their names from Saxon times. For example:
- *bourne* or *burn* means stream
- *burch* means large village
- *den* means pig pasture
- *ford* means a shallow part of a river where it could be crossed
- *ham* means village
- *ton* means a farm or small village
- *ley* means a clearing in the forest
- *ing* means people.

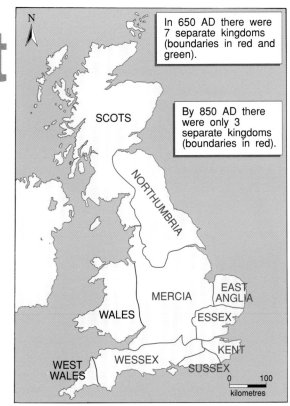

In 650 AD there were 7 separate kingdoms (boundaries in red and green).

By 850 AD there were only 3 separate kingdoms (boundaries in red).

SCOTS

NORTHUMBRIA

MERCIA

WALES

EAST ANGLIA

ESSEX

WEST WALES

WESSEX

KENT

SUSSEX

0   100
kilometres

The Saxon kingdoms in Britain.

Saxon settlements

This unit gives a clue on how to tell a Saxon town or village today.

1. On a map of Britain try to find ten towns which were built in Saxon times.
2. What did the towns and villages look like?

A chief's hall with log walls and a separate sleeping room on the side.

The towns and villages of Saxon Britain were much smaller than ours today - a village may have been only several cottages or huts. They were built very close to each other. Archaeologists have discovered traces of these houses which help them work out what the buildings might have looked like.

Saxon life

Read the unit carefully.

1. Describe what life might have been like in a Saxon village or town. Use the words below to help you.
   - healthy
   - comfortable
   - cold
   - draughty
   - warm
   - clean
   - safe
   - unhealthy
   - difficult
   - loving
   - hygienic
   - uncomfortable
   - damp
   - dingy
   - stuffy
   - pleasant
   - smelly
   - convenient

2. Explain how a Saxon house was made and what materials were used.

An ordinary peasant's hut with wattle and daub walls.

A slave's or poor person's hut sunk in the ground with a turf roof.

The walls were made from wooden planks and the roofs were thatched or turfed. They were usually rectangular in shape. One building was called the hall and was owned by the noble or chief. In large villages or towns there may have been several halls. In the hall, people gathered together to eat in the evenings. In the centre there would have been a stone-lined trench with a fire for cooking but mainly for warmth. There were no windows, so the only light came from the open door during the day and from wooden torches and the fire at night.

Tie Beams

Hearth: Clay Pad on Wooden Floor

Pit

Joist

What has helped archaeologists find out how a Saxon hut was built?

Smaller houses were used as workshops by the craftsmen, farmers and peasants. They were much simpler than the hall in style. Half of a hut was used as a stable for oxen, pigs, chickens and dogs. Animals would often roam freely around the living quarters. The hut might have a few stools and a wooden chest for clothes. Saxons probably did not own anything except their cooking utensils and the tools they needed for work.

**Land for 2 ploughs.
12 villagers and 7 small
holders have 5 ploughs.
Woodland pastures
1 league long and
1 wide.**

9. Saxon Farmers

The Saxons were farmers. Surrounding the village might have been two or three very large fields.

The fields were ploughed in long strips by a team of oxen pulling a heavy plough. Each farmer had a number of strips scattered among the large fields, so he had his share of good and poor soil. The fields were used to grow wheat and oats. Sometimes they were left for a year to let the soil recover.

Surrounding the fields there might have been woodland, useful for gathering fuel, herbs, berries, nuts and food for pigs, and containing wildlife for hunting. Waste grass and bushes were used as grazing for sheep and cows. Vegetable plots grew cabbages, beans and herbs close to the village. Streams, lakes and rivers provided another food source. It is very probable that bees were kept for honey to make mead (a sweet beer) and to sweeten food. In addition, Saxons were great hunters, especially good at hunting with hawks.

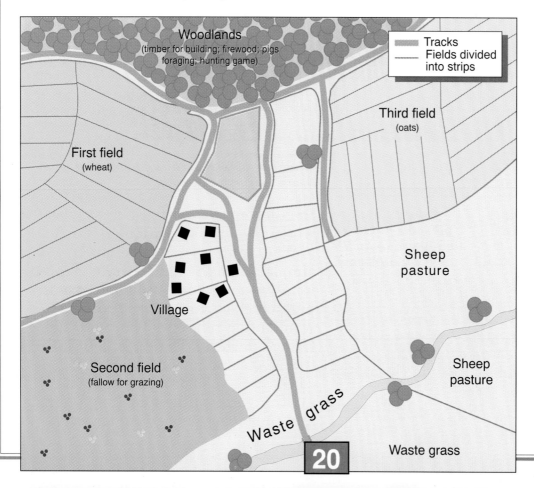

Woodlands
(timber for building; firewood; pigs foraging; hunting game)

Tracks
Fields divided into strips

Third field
(oats)

First field
(wheat)

Sheep pasture

Village

Second field
(fallow for grazing)

Sheep pasture

Waste grass

Waste grass

Saxon farmers worked from dawn until dusk throughout the year. Life was hard and rough.

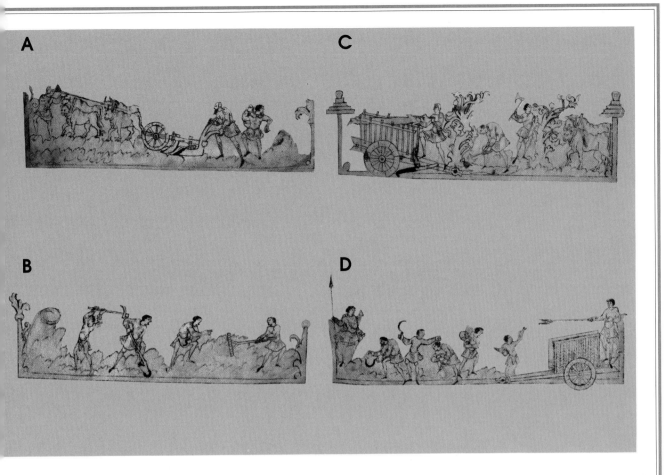

A

C

B

D

What work is being done on the farm in January (A), March (B), June (C) and August (D)?

Life was hard for the Saxons - even kings and queens. There were no hospitals or doctors, so people died of small wounds and illnesses. Men lived to the age of about 40, but women only lived to 35 because pregnancy was dangerous and frequent. One in three children died before the age of 10.

The diet was poor and limited. If there had been a bad harvest there was a risk of starvation. There were no shops where they could buy food if they ran out. If animals were sick because of plagues, this meant less food and fewer clothes. The poorer people only owned one set of clothes.

Saxon farming

Look at the pictures from a Saxon calendar showing how the land was farmed.

1. For each picture describe what you think is happening.
2. Describe the tools that are being used, the clothes and any machinery there is.

Living standards

Use the information in this unit.

1. Write down the important points about Saxon living standards.
2. Compare each point with life today. How have standards of living changed since Saxon times, for people living in Britain?

And in his honour they buried rings and brooches, cups and salvers in that barrow. They bequeathed every piece of shining gold to the earth and there it still remains, untouched by man.

10.

Imagine a journey on a Saxon longboat.

Sutton Hoo

In 1939 an archaeologist called Basil Brown began investigating a large, low, circular mound near the river Deben in Suffolk. Inside he discovered the outline of a magnificent Anglo-Saxon ship together with riches and wealth that made this the greatest British archaeological find ever.

In the centre of the ship was a burial chamber big enough to contain a huge coffin and all the belongings of someone important. In Saxon times it was believed that a king, a prince or great warrior needed all his belongings for his "new life" in the "next world" - a sort of heaven. All the belongings would have been put in the chamber after the whole ship had been dragged from the river and laid in a trench. Then the ship would have been covered to form a huge mound. The ship would have been the person's tomb. The mystery of Sutton Hoo is that no evidence of a body was found!

None of the wood or iron rivets that held the wooden planks together remained - they had all rotted away, leaving only stains in the sand. However, this was enough evidence to tell the archaeologist about the shape of the boat, how it was built and how it was powered.

What was found?

Look carefully at the remains found in the central chamber of the Sutton Hoo.

1. Make a list of all the objects found.
2. What type of person might these belong to? The words below might help you.

man	commoner
woman	priest
rich	warrior
poor	scholar
royalty	craftsman

3. In your own words, tell the story of the ceremony and burial of the Sutton Hoo ship and its owner.

Remains from the Sutton Hoo found buried in the sand.

The Sutton Hoo outline left in the sand.

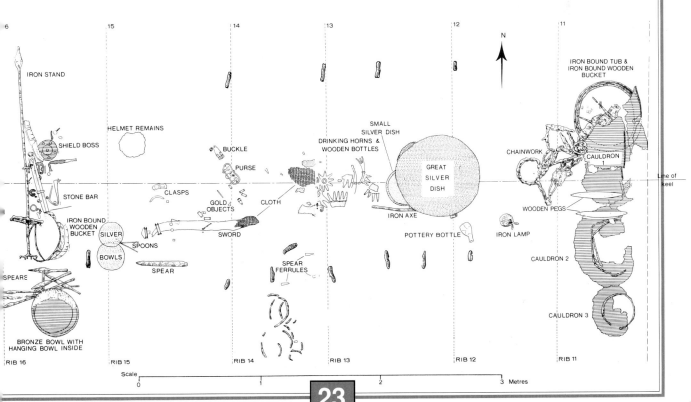

Pope Gregory the Great.

11.
Pagans and Christians

The first Saxon settlers were pagans. This means they worshipped many gods, such as Woden the chief of the gods, Thor the god of thunder, Frey the god of rain and crops and Tiw the god of battle. The Saxons were also very superstitious and believed in elves, goblins and dragons. The wealthier Saxons wore rings with secret letters and symbols carved on them. They believed these would protect them from danger and sickness. Archaeologists have also discovered evidence of human sacrifices and other offerings to the gods.

Many Romans and Britons were Christians before the Saxons came and they fled to Ireland for safety. People called missionaries later came back to try to teach the people about Jesus Christ. St. Patrick was a missionary.

A book called the *Anglo Saxon Chronicle* tells us that in AD 596 the Pope of Rome, Gregory, sent some monks to try and convert the Saxons in Britain to Christianity. They landed in Kent where the king, Ethelbert, was a pagan but his wife, Bertha, was a Christian. Soon many people, including Ethelbert, were baptised as Christians. The word of God spread to the Saxons living in other kingdoms.

The Saxons had their own alphabet. The letters were called runes and some have been engraved on this ring.

In AD 563 Columba, an Irish monk, together with his followers sailed to a small Scottish island called Iona. Here they built a small monastery. They were able to tell the people of Scotland about Christianity.

In AD 632 Oswald became king of Northumbria. He had spent some time in Iona and became a Christian. He sent for some monks to help convert the people of Northumbria to Christianity. One of those monks, Aidan, built a monastery on the island of Lindisfarne, just off the coast of Northumbria. Lindisfarne is now known as Holy Island.

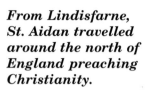

From Lindisfarne, St. Aidan travelled around the north of England preaching Christianity.

The Celtic Christians - Oswald and Columba - and the Roman Christians led by Augustine worshipped the same god but had different rules. They could not agree, for example, on the date for Easter. A meeting was held where they finally agreed on the Roman date. Most Saxon Christians then looked to Rome as the centre of their religion.

Although they were the last to be converted in Western Europe, the Saxons produced remarkable writers like Bede, carved ornate crosses and wrote and illustrated the stories of the Bible. These were written in beautiful illuminated manuscripts.

Today, Iona Abbey attracts visitors and still spreads Christianity.

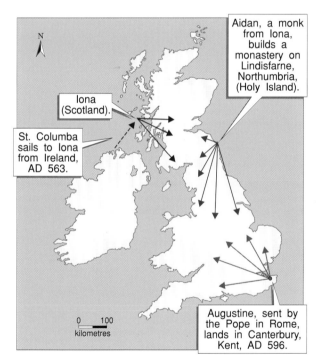

Aidan, a monk from Iona, builds a monastery on Lindisfarne, Northumbria, (Holy Island).

Iona (Scotland).

St. Columba sails to Iona from Ireland, AD 563.

0   100
kilometres

Augustine, sent by the Pope in Rome, lands in Canterbury, Kent, AD 596.

Christian monasteries in Saxon Britain.

 Saxon religions

By adding the word "day" to the names of the Saxon gods, you will find the names of certain days of the week.

1. Which are they?
2. Make a map showing the parts of Britain converted to Christianity.

12. Alfred the Great

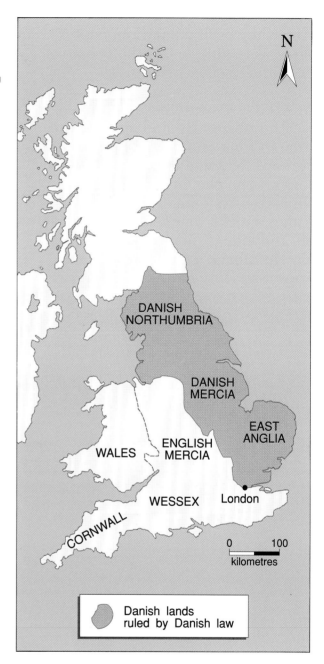

Danelaw - the result of the treaty between Alfred and Guthrum.

Success or failure for a Saxon king depended on how he dealt with the Vikings, who came from Denmark. At the time of Alfred's reign (AD 871 to 899) England was constantly fighting off Danish invasions. The Danes were capturing most of England and Alfred's army was beaten again and again.

With a few faithful followers Alfred retreated to the marshes of Somerset. Here he gathered an army together to fight against Guthrum and the Danes.

 At dawn Alfred attacked. Bishop Asser says:

He attacked the whole Danish army fighting furiously and by God's will eventually won the victory and made great slaughter among them.

Following the battle a peace treaty was arranged and Guthrum was even baptised. The North and East were ruled by the Vikings who called their land Danelaw. The South and West were ruled by Saxons.

Alfred

Read all the information about Alfred.

1. Why is Alfred called "Alfred the Great"?
2. What do you think were Alfred's greatest strengths, his brilliant military mind or his achievements for his country?
3. Write down Alfred's achievements. Say which you think are the most important.
4. If you were made king or queen today, what would you do to improve your country?

Alfred the Great. Do you carry anyone's picture around with you? Who do we show on our coins today?

Alfred the Great and his advisors.

First, Alfred defended towns by building walls and ditches so that people felt safer. He improved the army and built England's first navy. Next he turned to education. He wanted more people to read and write and even set up a school in his royal palace. He ordered his bishops to translate the Latin books into English so more people could read them. He took the most just laws from other areas and rewrote them for his kingdom. He was a wise ruler.

Alfred's achievements

Look carefully at the picture from an old manuscript.

1. Who do you think the people are?
2. What is happening in the picture?

He saw the Danish Queen entering the hall: purple gown, and long grey hair, and violet eyes. She swept up to the dais, and there the thane put the adorned cup into her hands.

13. Saxon Lifestyle

The Saxons were fond of feasting and entertaining. Banquets were held for families in the great hall. Archaeologists have discovered a Saxon settlement in Sussex and found the remains of animals and crops. These give us an idea of their diet. The remains included bones from pigs, sheep, chickens, goats, cattle, fish, deer and geese, and wild fruit seeds, peas, barley and wheat.

Food for the feast was probably prepared in outbuildings or cooked in cauldrons in the fire pit in the centre of the hall. Other than a knife there was no cutlery. People ate with their fingers and mopped up gravy or juices with bread. They drank out of drinking horns and special glass beakers which would not stand up on the tables. They had to be either emptied in one go or passed around until they were empty.

What would these objects be used for during a feast?

Would your life be difficult if you had to wear Saxon clothes? If so, why?

Archaeologists have discovered fragments of clothing which provide clues about what the Saxons wore. Manuscripts also provide evidence of the costumes worn.

Women's clothing was made of wool or linen and was simple for rich and poor. Richer women probably wore finer materials and also ornaments and jewellery. The clothes consisted of a long tunic over which was worn a long simple dress to the floor. Around her shoulders a Saxon woman wore a cloak fastened with a brooch (buttons and zips had not been invented). Over her head she wore a hood called a wimple. From a belt at her waist some key-shaped ornaments hung down. Their use is uncertain, but archaeologists think that they may have been to show that the woman was in charge of the household.

The men wore a knee-length tunic made of wool or linen. A cloak was worn over the top which was fastened with a brooch. Their legs were covered by breeches which were cross-gartered with leather thongs. Shoes were made of leather - if they had any. Manuscript pictures show Saxon men barefoot, even in winter!

 Then and now

Read this unit carefully.

1. What evidence has been found which tells us what the Saxons' diet was like?
2. Look at the picture of the feast and of Saxon articles. Describe the differences and similarities between meals in Saxon times and today. You could draw pictures to show the points.
3. Look at the pictures of Saxon clothes. How are they different from your own clothes?
4. What are your clothes made from? Which ones would the Saxons not have had?

In this year fierce, foreboding omens came over the land of Northumbria, and wretchedly terrified the people.

14. The Vikings Strike

The Viking raid at Lindisfarne was just the beginning. Not long afterwards they also raided monasteries at Iona and Jarrow. They burned the villages, killed women, children and monks, stole cattle and took the men as slaves. Most of all, they wanted the treasures of the monastery: the beautiful gold and silver cups, bowls and ornaments. The sight of Viking ships struck terror into the hearts of the Saxons; it signalled violence and robbery.

The year is AD 793 and the *Anglo Saxon Chronicle* records the first ever raid on Britain's shores by the Vikings:

There were excessive whirlwinds, lightning storms, and fiery dragons were seen flying in the sky. These signs were followed by great famine, and shortly afterwards in the same year, on January 8th, the raging of heathen men destroyed God's church at Lindisfarne through brutal robbery and slaughter.

The Lindisfarne stone showing Viking warriors making their attack. What weapons were used?

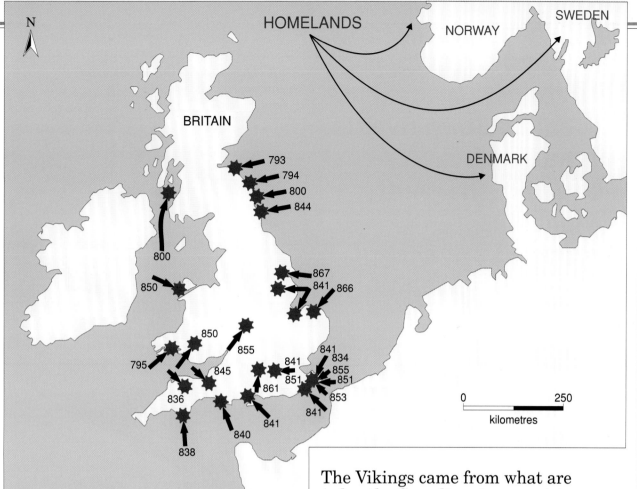

Points along the coast where the Vikings attacked Britain. Read the dates carefully to understand their plan.

In the beginning the Vikings raided for treasure, cattle and slaves. But as the raids grew in number and frequency, it became clear that the Vikings wanted to stay for good. Their shallow-hulled boats were able to sail on the rivers inland, or else they marched, built camps and stayed for the winter and then went home in the spring. By AD 850 they had decided to settle for good. They pushed their way across the country, built fortified villages and were able to defeat any local Saxon army that stood against them. Eventually they held more than half the country.

One reason why the Vikings came to stay was probably a shortage of good farming land in their homelands.

The Vikings came from what are today the Scandinavian countries - Norway, Sweden and Denmark. In those days, Sweden was covered in dense forest, Denmark had vast areas of heathland unsuitable for farming and Norway was very mountainous. England was a rich country plentiful in farming land and living space.

The Vikings were fierce warriors, but they were also great travellers and explorers, expert ship builders and navigators, peaceful farmers, merchants and traders, and marvellous craftsmen.

? Viking raiders

Use the information in this unit to help you.

1. Why did the Vikings come to England?
2. Imagine you are a Viking raider. Describe an attack on a monastery.

I watched the ship, my
    lady,
Launched down river to
    the ocean;
See where the great
    longship
Proudly lies at anchor,
Above the prow, the
    dragon
Rears its glowing head;
The bows were bound
    with gold
After the hull has
    launched.

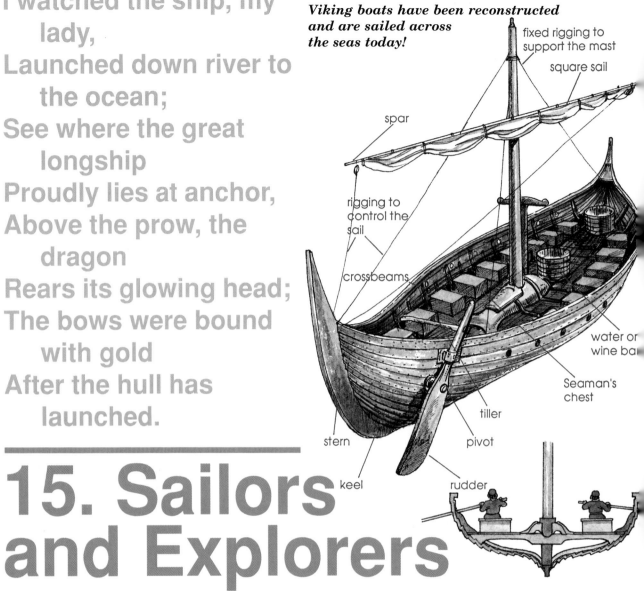

Viking boats have been reconstructed and are sailed across the seas today!

fixed rigging to support the mast

square sail

spar

rigging to control the sail

crossbeams

water or wine ba

Seaman's chest

tiller

stern

pivot

keel

rudder

15. Sailors and Explorers

The Vikings were expert sailors and boat builders and this allowed them to travel long distances by sea. There were different kinds of boats: warships, merchant ships for carrying cargo, fishing boats, coasters and rowing boats. A number of these boats have been discovered by archaeologists. This has given us some idea of the Vikings' expertise as sailors and navigators and about the seaworthiness of their vessels.

The longship was a Viking warship. These boats were about 20-25 metres long with a single mast and a big square sail. They held up to 40 men. When necessary the men rowed sitting on chests which held their personal belongings. Holes in the side of the ship allowed the oars through. The prow of the ship was often carved as a dragon's head and brightly painted. The ships were given names like "sea dragon" and "long serpent".

At the top of the mast might have been a bronze weather vane to show the Vikings the direction of the wind so they could set sail accordingly. A rudder guided the direction of the ship. The ships were built with overlapping planks nailed to frames. The joints between the planks were stuffed with rope and daubed in tar to make them watertight. Fresh drinking water was kept in barrels.

The Viking traders and explorers needed a different kind of ship from the fast, raiding longships. Merchant ships were shorter at only 16 metres long, but they were wider and deeper. They had decks at the bow and stern with space below for personal possessions and cargo and an open hold in the centre of the ship for larger cargoes and livestock. Space also had to be left for sleeping below decks on long voyages.

Viking ships are shown on picture stones.

Sea power was vital to the success of Viking trading and exploration. Today, modern Scandinavian rowing boats have the same design as Viking ships. This shows the quality of the old design.

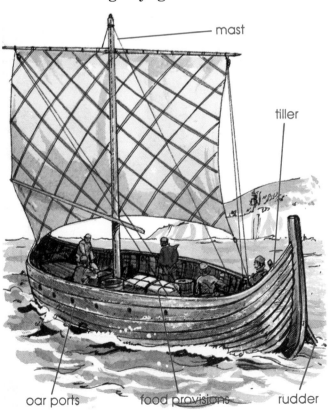

mast

tiller

oar ports   food provisions   rudder

A Viking cargo ship. This was too heavy to row and used one square sail.

Viking ships

Use the information in this unit.

1. Draw pictures of a longship and a trading merchant ship. Label the different parts of the ships.
2. How were the two ships different?
3. How do we know about the design of Viking ships? Why was the design so good?

These Viking sailing objects were found by archaeologists. What do you think they were used for?

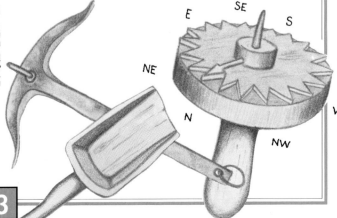

33

> "Such fear in my blood!" cried Odin. "I so long to range far and wide."

16. At Home and Abroad

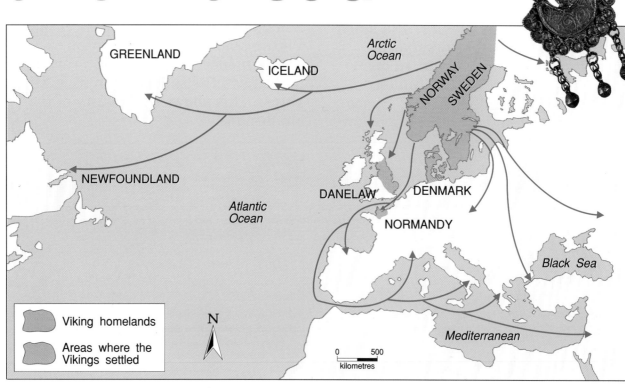

From their homelands of Norway, Sweden and Denmark the Vikings travelled to, explored, attacked and traded with many countries. The seas and great rivers of Europe were the highways for their longships and trading vessels. They settled in parts of Britain, Ireland and France. The part of France they settled in is called Normandy today, which means "Men from the North".

Which countries did the Vikings visit?

The Vikings sailed across the Atlantic Ocean to Iceland, Greenland and North America. In Europe they also sailed to Spain, Italy, Greece and Israel. To the east they sailed down the great rivers of Europe to Russia.

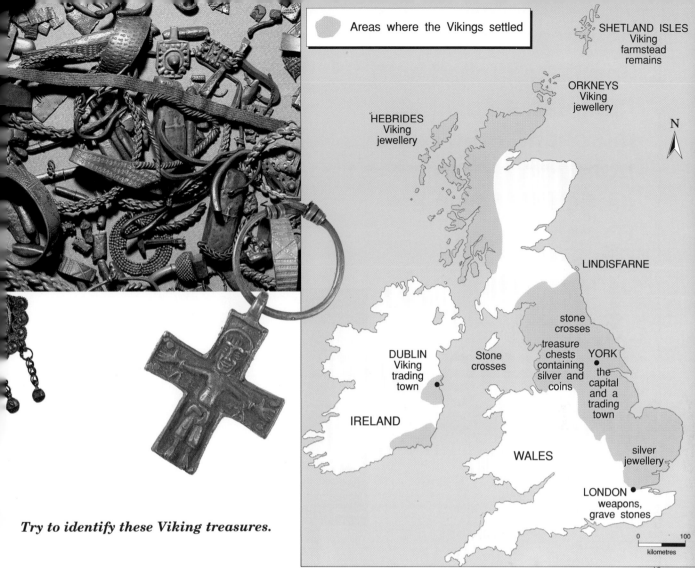

Try to identify these Viking treasures.

Evidence remaining today from the Vikings living in Britain.

The Vikings took goods from their homelands to trade in the new countries: fox, sable, squirrel and beaver furs, amber, dried fish, honey, ivory (from walrus tusks), walrus hides (for rope making), antler bone and whale oil.

They wanted to swap their goods for: silver (ornaments, jewellery and coins), wood, wheat, wine, spices, pottery, slaves and glass. These things were hard to find in their home countries.

The *Anglo Saxon Chronicle* tells us when and where the Vikings attacked and raided. Other evidence tells us where they settled - such as place names, Viking stone crosses, jewellery, remains of farmhouses or other dwellings and weapons.

The Vikings controlled a large part of the North and part of England which was called Danelaw.

 Viking travellers

Look carefully at this unit to help you.

1. What goods did the Vikings take with them, and what did you receive in return?
2. If you had lived in these times, where would you have liked to travel?
3. Why do you think the Vikings were such brave travellers?

Jorvik - enriched with the treasure of merchants who came from all quarters, particularly from the Danish people.

17. Vikings in York

The archaeologists have been able to reconstruct the town from the evidence they have found. You may be lucky enough to go and see this for yourself.

The houses were made of timber, with thatched roofs and packed very closely together.

Once the Vikings had conquered the north of England, many settled and traded from the town of York. They called it Jorvik and it became the capital of their kingdom.

Excavations by archaeologists in 1977 revealed the importance of the capital. They found the remains of buildings, craftsmen's workshops and articles beautifully preserved in the wet mud. These tell us that Jorvik was both a local and an international trading centre and a very wealthy one. They also tell us what the town's people wore, what jobs they did, how they lived, what they ate and how they spent their spare time.

Many leather items were discovered, such as boots, shoes, belts, purses and bags. Here is the leather stall in the market. The man on the right has been suffering from shoes that are too tight.

Two shops close together - an antler worker who made combs and comb cases and a wood turner who made bowls, cups, buckets, stools and tool handles.

Inside one of the houses a meal is being prepared for the family.

The Vikings had to make their own clothes. The mother is spinning wool into yarn, while the children watch and learn. There is a loom for weaving cloth. There were no schools in Viking times, but children were expected to do chores and tasks from an early age.

The river was an important part of the town. At the harbour ships moored up and loaded and unloaded goods like furs, skins, wine and fish.

 ## Life in Jorvik

Read the information and look at the pictures carefully.

1. Describe the inside and outside of a Viking town house. How is it different from your own house?
2. Describe the town's market shops. In what ways was shopping different in Viking times? If you needed change, silver coins were cut up!
3. What jobs do you do in your home? How is your life different from that of a Viking girl or boy?
4. Would you have liked to live in Jorvik in the 10th century?

They were fair-haired and red faced. I notice that some of them had bracelets and other pieces of jewellery, and some had embroidered cloaks.

Sometimes brooches to fasten a tunic were joined by a chain.

18.
Viking Clothes

It would be very interesting to go back in time to see real Viking women and men. Unfortunately this is not possible, but there is evidence to find out about their clothes, jewellery, footwear and hairstyles.

Fragments of cloth, jewellery, leather boots and shoes, bags and belts show us what materials were used and how they were made. There are descriptions of Viking dress in stories and poems.

The Vikings made pictures of themselves on carvings and embroideries. These give us an idea of how they looked.

We know that Viking women had long, linen dresses reaching almost to the ground. These were either plain or pleated. On top of the dress they wore a long, woollen tunic that looked a bit like an apron. This was held up by a pair of brooches. Over this there would be a shawl or cloak fastened by a pin or brooch. Leather shoes were worn.

Other brooches were worn on a dress or shawl.

Men liked to show off their appearance with fine clothing and jewellery. Clothing was made of linen or wool but silk fragments have also been found. Cloth was dyed in attractive colours using vegetable juices. The men wore trousers held up by a sash around the waist. A tunic was worn over the top with a belt. In winter, men wore overcloaks held with brooches or pins. On their feet they wore shoes or ankle boots made of leather.

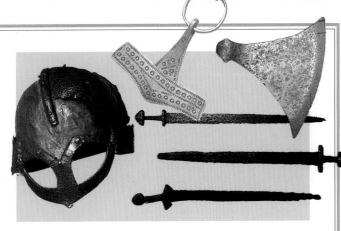

A sword was a treasured possession and often given a special name.

All men carried weapons - daggers, spears or swords. In battle they were very courageous. Their favourite weapons were the axe and spear. They defended themselves with large round wooden shields which were often painted in bright colours. The more wealthy chieftains wore helmets made of iron and chain mail to protect themselves.

Finger and arm rings were popular.

Leather shoes.

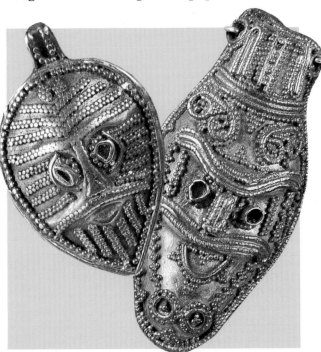

Sometimes a special pendant was worn which was supposed to have magic powers for protection.

? Viking dress

Read this unit carefully.

1. How do we know about Viking dress and jewellery?
2. Make a list of the clothes you wear to school and at home. How are they different from those of a Viking?
3. Sometimes Vikings were buried fully clothed with their personal possessions. If you were buried with your favourite things what would they be? What would people in the future know about you from the goods they would find? What would they not know about you?

Man for man they seemed bigger than the English ... but for the most part there was no great show of luxury about them, such as I had expected. Indeed they had a rather plain, working day appearance.

19. Viking Lifestyle

Describe the Vikings' dress for men and women.

The Vikings had a bad reputation because of their raiding and plundering. They were certainly fearsome and brave warriors. But most Vikings were peaceful farmers, skilled and artistic craftsmen and wealthy merchants. They were also courageous explorers and travellers who sailed vast distances in beautiful ships and used clever navigational aids.

Although the Vikings were quarrelsome, they believed in law and order. They held an assembly called the Althing, which was a mixture of a law court and a parliament. Here, laws were made after discussion and punishments were given to wrongdoers.

 Viking life

Look at the evidence in this unit.

1. Why did the Vikings have a bad reputation? Do you believe it was unfair? What evidence is there to suggest it was fair?
2. What was the Althing? How do we settle disagreements today?
3. List the jobs of Viking women. Do you think it would have been good or bad to be a woman in Viking times?
4. Write down three ways in which Vikings buried their dead.
5. Elsewhere in this book you will read more about what Vikings believed happened to them after they died. Find out as much as you can about the Viking gods and Valhalla.

Women were responsible for all the household duties, such as cooking, cleaning, washing and caring for the children. They made clothes by spinning, weaving and dying cloth. They would have learned the skills as children and in turn also taught their children. In this way the traditions and the customs of the people were passed on. There were no schools for Viking children! While doing their chores, children listened to stories, poems and songs about their people.

The King or Chief
King Court, Harold Bluetooth and Swein Forkleard were 3 famous Viking kings.

The Karls
They were rich freemen and farmers.

The Jarls
They owned land and were probably skilled craftsmen and merchants.

The Thralls or slaves
Their owners had the power of life and death over them.

In many countries at this time women were expected to be obedient to their husbands and fathers, as if they were owned by them. Viking women could be independent. Although fathers were responsible for choosing a husband for their daughters, girls were rarely forced to marry men they did not like. They could also divorce their husband if they wished. They were allowed to own land, to farm and trade, especially if they were wealthy. For many women life was hard - half the women died by the age of 35, and 55 was considered "old-age"!

The kings and chiefs were the most important Vikings. They were buried in their ships together with their personal possessions and best clothes. The whole ship was buried under a mound of earth. These burial mounds have helped us to understand how the Vikings lived and died. Sometimes, Vikings and their possessions were cremated (burned) and the ashes buried. For less important Vikings, a simple form of burial was more common. They were usually buried unburned in the earth with their tools, weapons and jewellery.

◄ *The Vikings' positions in society.*

What was buried with this Viking? ▼

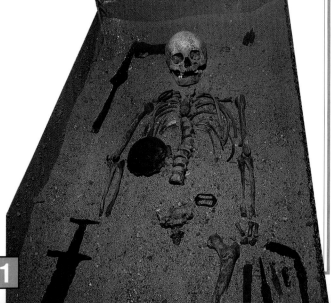

There came the unwelcome report that the land of England had lost its King, and that Harold had been crowned in his stead.

The last hours of Edward's life.

20. Towards Invasion in 1066

Edward the Confessor.

Edward the Confessor was the last Anglo-Saxon king. He had ruled for 23 years and by 1065 he was dying. Edward was a very religious man and was responsible for building Westminster Abbey. He spent a good deal of his later life praying and telling God of his sins. This is why he is called "Edward the Confessor". He had no sons to follow him as king.

Edward had strong bonds with Normandy. Before he became king of England he had lived there. His mother, Emma, was the daughter of the Duke of Normandy. Before he died Edward promised William, Duke of Normandy, that he would be the next king. On 5th January, 1066 Edward died. Edward's death plunged England into turmoil which

The coronation of Harold.

The Bayeux Tapestry

Look at this picture from the Bayeux Tapestry. It shows the last hours of Edward's life.

1. In the top part of the picture find:
   - Edward's wife, Queen Edith;
   - the King himself;
   - Harold Goodwin, Earl of Wessex (kneeling);
   - Archbishop Stigand.
2. Look at the bottom part of the picture. What do you think has happened?

eventually resulted in the Norman invasion and the Battle of Hastings in 1066. It was Harold Goodwin, Earl of Wessex, who was to travel to Normandy to promise William the Crown. He had done this by swearing on holy relics. But when Edward died, the English Council elected Harold king because he was English, a strong ruler of Wessex and a good warrior.

The *Anglo Saxon Chronicle* tells us that "Earl Harold was crowned King and he had little peace during the time he ruled the Kingdom". Harold knew that if he wanted to keep the Crown he would have to fight for it. When William in Normandy received the news it is said he became silent, his face black with fury. The king of Norway, Harold Hardrada, also believed that he had a claim to the throne because his wife was a descendant of an old king of England. Both made preparations for war.

Three powerful men thought they should be king. Who was to win?

Claimants to the throne

Read about the fight for the crown once Edward had died.

1. Look at the picture of Harold being crowned and describe the event.
2. Who do you think has most claim to the throne? Why?
3. What was the cause of all the trouble? What do you think will be the result?

William arrived with a countless host of horsemen, slingers, archers and foot soldiers.

The Normans attack the English.

21. August to October 1066

Harold arranged his army around him on the ridge of a hill and prepared for the Norman attack. The battle began at nine in the morning, with about 8 000 on each side. First, the Norman archers with their short bows opened fire, but the Saxons stopped them with their shields. Next, the Norman foot soldiers advanced and were met by a ferocious hail of missiles. Then the hand-to-hand fighting started. The Saxons severely beat the Normans who had to retreat!

Things were going badly for William. He decided to launch an attack with his mounted knights. Again they suffered heavy losses and had to retreat. Thinking the battle was won, the Saxons left the hill to pursue the Normans. But the Normans on the flatter ground fought back, and caused heavy casualties on the Saxon side. This weakened the part of the Saxon army which was still grouped around Harold's standard on the hilltop.

? The Battle of Hastings

Read carefully about the battle in this unit.

1. Draw a chart like this:

Harold's army		William's army	
Advantages	Disadvantages	Advantages	Disadvantages

List the advantages and disadvantages each army had.
2. Who do you think had the greatest claim to the throne of England - Harold, William or Harold Hardrada?
3. Using the Bayeux Tapestry to help you, draw pictures of the Saxon soldiers and Norman knights. Describe their weapons and armour.

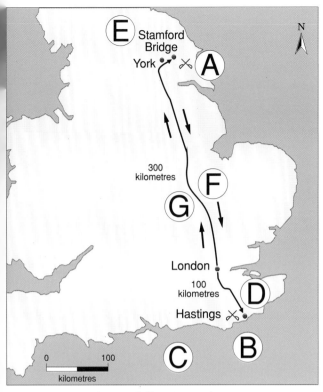

The path of Harold's campaign.

The battle wore on into the afternoon. Again William used his archers to weaken the Saxons. This time the arrows found their mark; Harold himself was wounded in the face by an arrow. The Norman knights now moved in. Two of Harold's brothers were killed and finally Harold himself was struck down. The remainder of the Saxon army fled - William was victorious!

Knights and archers on their way.

The battle

Think about the conditions of the battle and imagine you are a soldier.

1. Decide whose side you are fighting for.
2. Write an account of your experiences.

On Christmas day 1066 William was crowned king of England in Westminster Abbey. Life in England was about to change ...

The battle for the crown

Look at the map on this page. Copy this table and match each letter on the map to the number.

1	King Harold knows that William will fight for the Crown. He prepares for the invasion by building a fleet of warships to defend the country. In August, fed up with waiting, Harold disbands his fleet.	
2	In September Harold Hardrada, a Viking, sails with 300 ships and invades the north of England. He reaches York.	
3	Hearing of the Viking invasion, Harold marches the English army north from London to meet the Vikings.	
4	On 25th September, at Stamford Bridge, two miles from York, the English fight the Vikings and destroy the invading army.	
5	On the 27th and 28th September, Duke William and the Norman invasion fleet land at Pevensey near Hastings.	
6	Harold receives news of this second invasion and is forced to march his tired army back to the south to Hastings.	
7	On October 14th, 1066 Harold's and William's armies face each other at Hastings in the final battle for the Crown of England.	

22. The Bayeux Tapestry

B

Here King Harold was killed, perhaps with an arrow in his eye.

What is the Bayeux Tapestry? First, it is not a tapestry at all. It is an embroidery of eight coloured wools: red, yellow or buff, grey, two shades of green and three shades of blue. The wool was stitched using a needle on to a background of linen. The embroidery is like a very long strip cartoon. It is 70 metres long but only 50 centimetres high. It is made up of eight pieces of linen skilfully stitched together, which tell the story leading up to and including the Battle of Hastings.

The story takes place from 1064 to 1066 and asks a question, "Who will be the next king of England when Edward the Confessor dies?" There are two parts.

Part 1
Edward sends Harold Goodwin of Wessex to France to see William. William is told that he will succeed Edward. Harold is captured by a local baron in France but William sets him free. Harold helps William fight a rebel and is richly rewarded. Harold swears on holy relics that he will help William to become king on Edward's death and returns to England. Edward dies on 5th January, 1066 and is buried in the newly built Westminster Abbey. The English Parliament wastes no time in finding a new king and **Harold** is crowned!

A

A comet terrifies the people.

The Bayeux Tapestry

Study the pictures in this unit.

1. Look at picture **A** from the Bayeux Tapestry and find:
   - the people, pointing to a comet over Harold's palace;
   - the newly crowned Harold being told that bad omens have been seen;
   - the ghostly invasion fleet beneath Harold's feet.
2. Which figure is Harold? Write in your own words how you think Harold died.

William the Conqueror

Read about how William was made king of England and study his portrait.

1. Design a panel for an embroidery to show his coronation on Christmas Day, 1066. Where will your embroidery be kept?

William I, 1066-1087.

Part 2

William, in France, receives news that Harold has accepted the crown. He gives the command for an invasion fleet to be built. The fleet is made ready and loaded with supplies and horses. The Norman army sets sail. The invasion fleet lands in England and on 14th October, 1066 the Norman and English armies clash at Hastings. By nightfall, after a vicious battle, Harold is killed! The remainder of the English army flees and on Christmas Day, 1066 Duke William of Normandy is crowned king of England in Westminster Abbey.

Index